Parenthood is about raising and celebrating the child you have, not the child you thought you would have. It is about understanding that your child is exactly the person they are supposed to be. And, if you are lucky, they might be the teacher who turns you into the person you are supposed to be.

— Joan Ryan

THIS IS WHAT AUTISM LOOKS LIKE

Understanding Behaviors in the Classroom
+ Activities

Written by Michelle Ucar
Illustrated by Alexandra Stepan

Julen, your approach to life is admirable . . . never a complaint or an argument. The challenges that you have endured have not laid burden on how you live your life. You take on each day without labels or limitations — not allowing a number, a letter or a word define you — and for that, I applaud you. The example that you set for kids, young adults, parents and family is one that I cannot teach, but one that I can learn from. Thank you!

♡ Mom

Written by Michelle Ucar
Illustrated by Alexandra Stepan

This Is What It Looks Like, Volume 1
Published in the United States, 2021.
©2021 Julen's Ausome Sauce
ISBN: 978-1-709779-21-3

Email: info@julensausomesauce.com
Website: www.julensausomesauce.com

All rights reserved. No part of this publication may be reproduced, stored in or introduced into a retrieval system, or transmitted in any form or by any means without prior written permission.

em·pa·thy

[em-puh-thee]

Noun

The ability to understand and share the feelings of another.

As a parent, our job is to love and protect our children. When they are faced with a challenge, our first instinct is to help them figure out how to overcome it. Some challenges require a great deal of creativity and perseverance. Even then, they are not necessarily "overcome" but they can become manageable.

This series of books was created by a group of moms who had to figure out a path for our children that would lead to independence and success. Each book is a compilation of daily events that describes the challenges of a special needs student as they successfully navigate those challenges in an inclusive classroom.

By sharing our stories, we hope to encourage acceptance, support inclusion and, most of all, promote empathy!

More in this Series

This Is What ADHD Looks Like
Oliver shares his experience with great passion and energy. You can feel the excitement on each page as you learn more about ADHD.

This Is What DYSLEXIA Looks Like
Samantha explains what it is like for her to learn with Dyslexia. She proves that with hard work and dedication, it is possible to master the skills needed to deal with her challenges.

This Is What BLIND Looks Like
Taylor takes you on her journey of conquering the classroom without sight. With the support of those around her, she teaches you how to see light in the darkness.

Children are unique. No two are alike.

This is an introduction to one child's journey.

Let's take a closer look at what autism looks like...

Every child with Autism is different . . . that is what makes us amazing! However, I want to tell you about a few challenges that are the same with many autistic children. If you are aware of these challenges, it might make it easier for all of us to be in the classroom together.

On the next few pages, I am going to help you understand more about me! My name is Julen and, just like you, I like having friends. I want you to know that it is okay to talk to me and ask me questions.

That's me!

Sometimes, I get very interested in a toy and I might play with it in a different way than you do. For example, I like to take all of the cars out of the bin and line them up side by side.

You might notice that I am really good at some things, but have difficulty with others. For instance, I can tell you the names and jersey numbers of all of the professional players in football, baseball and soccer. However, I have a hard time holding my pencil the right way . . . so my handwriting is not very neat.

I can talk, but I do not always use complete sentences. There are kids like me who are non-verbal and they cannot express themselves with words, but that does not mean that they do not understand. Try to relate to them in another way. They could be great at drawing or they might be able to build amazing things out of Lego bricks!

I have trouble with social interactions. This means that if you say "Hi!" I might not say it back. I am not mad at you, I just do not always know how to respond.

I also have strong reactions to one or more of the senses:
- I like to touch, but I do not like to be touched
- Loud noises are painful for me to hear
- Seeing too many shapes and colors in the classroom makes it hard for me to focus
- The texture and taste of food can bother me

For the most part, I am a happy kid. If I do get upset, it may take a while for me to get over it. The best way for you to deal with this is to leave me alone or find an adult who can help.

A change in routine might upset me. For this reason, I like to have a visual schedule on my desk. This is a set of pictures that I use to plan out each day. If something is going to change, I swap out the picture and talk about it with my teacher. This way, there are no surprises.

There will be times when I rock back and forth in my chair or flap my hands. This is called stimming, which means that I repeat the same physical motion over and over as a way to calm myself during stressful situations. To reduce the amount that I move, I like to sit on a wedge-shaped cushion that I call a "wiggle seat." This helps so that I do not disrupt my classmates.

Most days I am called out of the classroom by other teachers and you might wonder why. Sometimes I am practicing reading and other times I am doing writing exercises. I am still learning, just in a different way. It helps me a lot if you let me know what we are working on when I get back!

I hope you have liked learning about me and find this helpful in understanding some of the behaviors of kids with autism. If you have questions, you can always ask your teacher or your parents. Just like you, I want to be accepted. Our differences make our classroom unique.

LOOK AT ME NOW

Continue the Conversation

Use the next section to engage your students in meaningful discussion. Photocopy as needed for in-class or at-home activities.

These activities give students the skills to understand and talk about our differences. They will learn positive and proactive strategies that support inclusion through self-kindness, friendliness, and empathy.

YOU CANNOT TEACH EMPATHY. YOU HAVE TO EXPERIENCE IT.

Activity 1

OBJECTIVE

To learn about autism in the classroom and increase each student's willingness and ability to be inclusive.

INSIGHTS

Inclusion is much larger than placement in the regular classroom. Just because an autistic student has a seat in the classroom, it does not mean that they feel included. The goal of inclusion is achieved only when every student is participating.

Every child with Autism is different... that is what makes us amazing! However, I want to tell you about a few challenges that are the same with many autistic children. If you are aware of these challenges, it might make it easier for all of us to be in the classroom together.

EMPATHY PROMPTS

What do you think having autism is like?

What does it mean to be inclusive?

How can you be more inclusive?

How would you feel if you were not included?

POST-ACTIVITY DISCUSSION

When students understand their own and other people's differences, it teaches them empathy and helps to build a stronger community.

It is not our differences that divide us. It is our inability to recognize, accept, and celebrate those differences.
　　　　　　　　　　　　　　　　　　~Audre Lorde

Inclusion

Think of creative ways that you can be inclusive.

Ben loves sports. What could you say to include him on your team?	Sarah always sits alone at lunch. What could you say to include her at your table?
_____	_____
_____	_____
_____	_____
_____	_____
James has a hard time interacting with the class. What could you say to include him in your group project?	Augie worries a lot. What could you say to make him feel better about the test on Friday?
_____	_____
_____	_____
_____	_____
_____	_____

Activity 2

OBJECTIVE

To respect the unique characteristics and behaviors of students with autism.

INSIGHTS

Feeling understood and supported is especially important for students with autism. It helps them stay motivated, increases self-awareness, and encourages them to advocate for themselves.

Sometimes I get very interested in a toy and I might play with it in a different way than you do. For example, I like to take all of the cars out of the bin and line them up side by side.

EMPATHY PROMPTS

What are some things you notice about students with autism?

Do these behaviors cause them to be excluded?

How do you think that makes them feel?

What could you do to help them feel better?

POST-ACTIVITY DISCUSSION

It's one thing to understand the importance of empathy, it's another thing to respond with empathy.

If students are encouraged to show empathy, they will begin to feel more confident expressing their feelings in a safe environment.

Empathy

Empathy means putting yourself in someone else's shoes to help understand how they might be feeling. In the following situations, how would you respond with empathy?

JENNY'S DOG RAN AWAY

How do you think she is feeling? _____

Have you ever felt this way before?   YES   NO

When you felt this way, what helped you feel better? _____

What do you think you can say or do to help Jenny feel better? _____

_____

EVAN FORGOT TO STUDY FOR HIS TEST

How do you think he is feeling? _____

Have you ever felt this way before?   YES   NO

When you felt this way, what helped you feel better? _____

What do you think you can say or do to help Evan feel better? _____

_____

LUCY TRIPPED AND FELL IN FRONT OF THE ENTIRE CLASS

How do you think she is feeling? _____

Have you ever felt this way before?   YES   NO

When you felt this way, what helped you feel better? _____

What do you think you can say or do to help Lucy feel better? _____

_____

Activity 3

OBJECTIVE

To realize the strengths of students with autism.

INSIGHTS

Autism is associated with specific strengths such as attention to detail, the ability to hyperfocus, good memory, and creativity.

> You might notice that I am really good at some things, but have difficulty with others. For instance, I can tell you the names and jersey numbers of all of the professional players in football, baseball and soccer. However, I have a hard time holding my pencil the right way . . . so my handwriting is not very neat.

EMPATHY PROMPTS

What strengths do you notice in students with autism?

How could they apply their strengths in the classroom?

What are some of your strengths?

POST-ACTIVITY DISCUSSION

Encourage students to talk about how they could use their strengths to help someone else.

Strengths

Fill out this chart to realize your strengths and identify areas where you may struggle.

	Strength?	Struggle?	Why?
SCHOOL			
Testing	☐	☐	
Homework	☐	☐	
Organization	☐	☐	
Class Subjects	☐	☐	
SELF ESTEEM			
School	☐	☐	
Peers	☐	☐	
Extra Ciricular	☐	☐	
RELATIONSHIPS			
Teacher	☐	☐	
Parent	☐	☐	
Sibling	☐	☐	
Peer	☐	☐	
Coach	☐	☐	
BEHAVIOR			
Empathy	☐	☐	
Honesty	☐	☐	
Kindness	☐	☐	
Acceptance	☐	☐	
Inclusion	☐	☐	
PHYSICAL			
Eating Habits	☐	☐	
Exercise	☐	☐	

Activity 4

OBJECTIVE

To acknowledge that there are many ways to communicate with autistic students, and it is not always verbal.

INSIGHTS

The development of conversation and social skills in the classroom is dependent upon opportunities for students to observe and participate with peers.

I can talk, but I do not always use complete sentences. There are kids like me who are non-verbal and they cannot express themselves with words, but that does not mean that they don't understand. Try to relate to them in another way. They could be great at drawing or they might be able to build amazing things out of Lego bricks!

EMPATHY PROMPTS

What are some non-verbal ways to communicate?

If someone doesn't understand you, what can you do differently?

What are some ways to start a conversation?

POST-ACTIVITY DISCUSSION

Communication is the act of transferring information from one person to another. Helping students choose an appropriate communication channel is important and requires understanding the difference between verbal and nonverbal communication.

Communication Skills

Think about different ways that you can include someone using verbal and non-verbal communication skills.
Sounds like (verbal) = "Do you want to play with us?"
Looks like (non-verbal) = Signaling with a wave and a smile

Practice the following:	Sounds like... (verbal)	Looks like... (non-verbal)
Ask someone to be your partner		
Encourage someone to talk in turn		
Include someone at the lunch table		

Activity 5

OBJECTIVE

To develop skills in order to communicate with autistic students.

INSIGHTS

Planning activities with a focus on conversation and social skills promotes positive interaction. These activities help autistic students to successfully communicate their wants and needs and nurture meaningful relationships with peers.

I have trouble with social interactions. This means that if you say "Hi!" I might not say it back. I am not mad at you, I just do not always know how to respond.

What's up, Julen?

Hi Julen!

EMPATHY PROMPTS

Have you ever greeted a classmate and they did not respond?

Did you try again?

What do you think made the difference?
(tone of voice, smile, the words, hand gesture)

What did you learn from this?

POST-ACTIVITY DISCUSSION

Individuals with autism struggle with communication skills and have difficulty understanding the give-and-take context necessary to create a conversation. It can be helpful to prepare students for conversations they might have in different social situations to support inclusion.

Conversation

Use this worksheet to prepare and practice your conversation skills with someone that might not respond. The speech bubbles give you an example of what you might say.

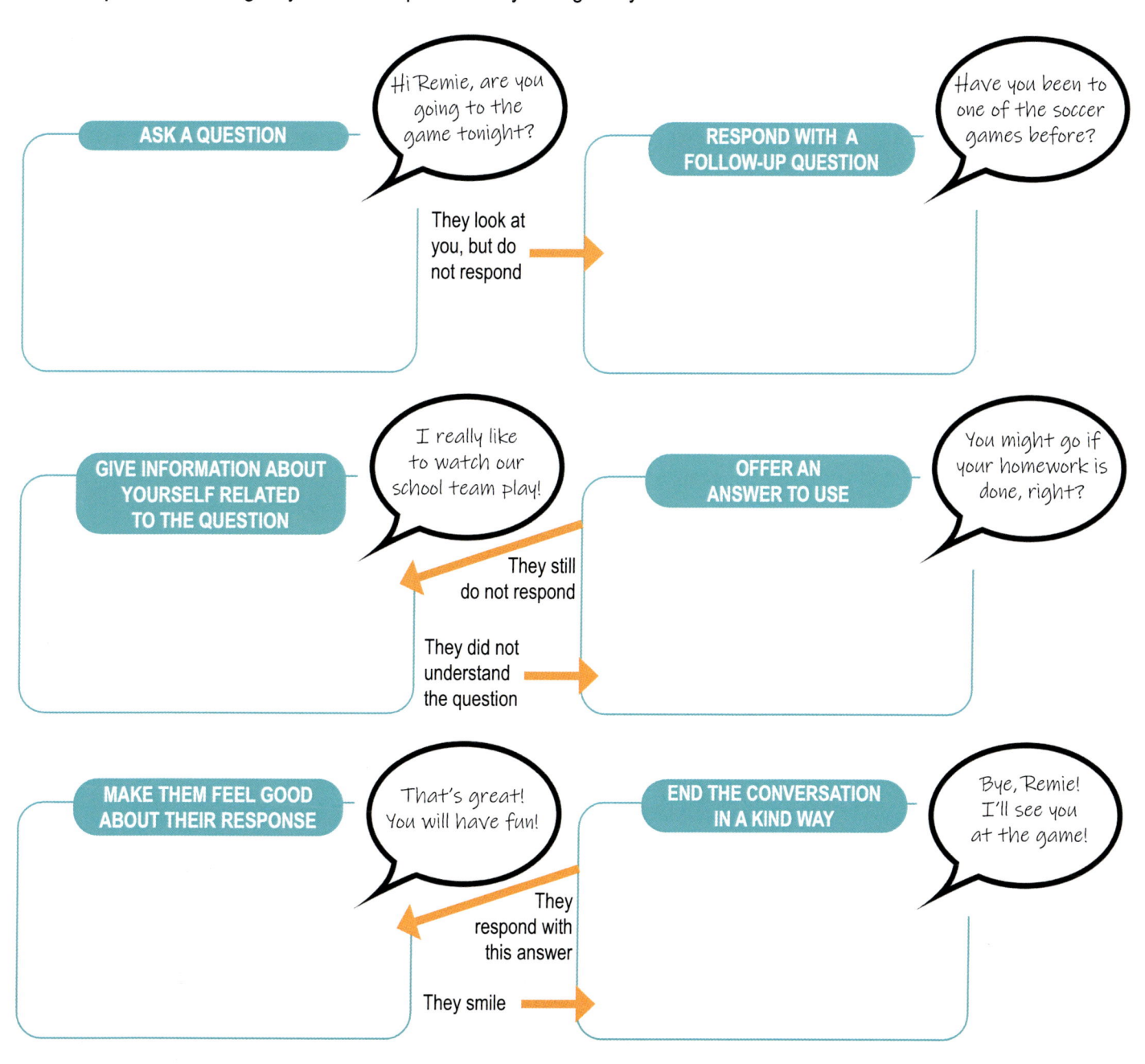

ASK A QUESTION

Hi Remie, are you going to the game tonight?

They look at you, but do not respond →

RESPOND WITH A FOLLOW-UP QUESTION

Have you been to one of the soccer games before?

GIVE INFORMATION ABOUT YOURSELF RELATED TO THE QUESTION

I really like to watch our school team play!

← They still do not respond

They did not understand the question →

OFFER AN ANSWER TO USE

You might go if your homework is done, right?

MAKE THEM FEEL GOOD ABOUT THEIR RESPONSE

That's great! You will have fun!

← They respond with this answer

They smile →

END THE CONVERSATION IN A KIND WAY

Bye, Remie! I'll see you at the game!

Activity 6

OBJECTIVE

To recognize and manage what causes anxiety in the classroom.

INSIGHTS

We all get anxious, but for someone with autism the feelings are sometimes stronger and can be overwhelming. Some things that might make someone with autism anxious are: being hugged or touched, loud noises, bright or flashing lights, or strong odors.

I also have strong reactions to one or more of the senses:
- *I like to touch, but I do not like to be touched*
- *Loud noises are painful for me to hear*
- *Seeing too many shapes and colors in the classroom makes it hard for me to focus*
- *The texture and taste of food can bother me*

EMPATHY PROMPTS

What is anxiety?

What do you do when you are feeling anxious?

Can you tell when someone is anxious?

How can you show empathy for someone who is experiencing anxiety?

POST-ACTIVITY DISCUSSION

Students on the autism spectrum experience anxiety because of difficulties they have with communication, predicting outcomes, understanding social interaction, and sensory processing. This activity can help to:

1. Reduce confusion and unpredictability
2. Increase a sense of calm

Anxiety

Recognize and manage anxiety in your classroom.

Things that make me feel anxious:

This is how my body reacts:

These are the thoughts that I have:

What can I do to manage my anxiety?

Activity 7

OBJECTIVE

To realize that students with autism have difficulty understanding and expressing emotion.

INSIGHTS

Recognizing an emotion depends largely on information from the eyes and mouth. Students with autism often avoid eye contact, so they do not receive facial cues, which contributes to their difficulty detecting emotions.

For the most part, I am a happy kid. If I do get upset, it may take a while for me to get over it. The best way for you to deal with this is to leave me alone or find an adult who can help.

EMPATHY PROMPTS

What are the different emotions?

How do you recognize an emotion?

What cues do you look for to determine how someone is feeling?

POST-ACTIVITY DISCUSSION

Students have just experienced how difficult it is for an autistic student to understand emotion. Imagine if you did not have cues to interpret the situation properly and had to guess at an emotional response.

Emotions

Describe what you think just happened to each person. Then, try to do the same thing when you cannot see their face.

What happened?

_____

What emotion does she feel?

_____

What happened?

_____

What emotion does he feel?

_____

What happened?

_____

What emotion does she feel?

_____

What happened?

_____

What emotion does he feel?

_____

What happened?

_____

What emotion does she feel?

_____

What happened?

_____

What emotion does he feel?

_____

Activity
8

OBJECTIVE

To appreciate the importance of a visual schedule for a student with autism.

INSIGHTS

Students with autism may feel anxious if expectations are not clearly understood or routines are not in place.

Visual schedules are a tool that can help students with autism follow a routine, transition between activities, and develop new skills.

A change in routine might upset me. For this reason, I like to have a visual schedule on my desk. This is a set of pictures that I use to plan out each day. If something is going to change, I swap out the picture and talk about it with my teacher. This way, there are no surprises.

EMPATHY PROMPTS

How could a visual schedule help you?

What types of activities would you include on your schedule?

Do you think a visual schedule would help your classmates understand your day better?

POST-ACTIVITY DISCUSSION

Posting a visual schedule in the classroom can calm anxieties, help students with transitioning, and help non-readers, ESL students and special education students know what is coming next.

Visual Schedule

Cut out pictures, draw your own, or write in each square the activities that make up your daily schedule. Use this as a visual reminder throughout your day.

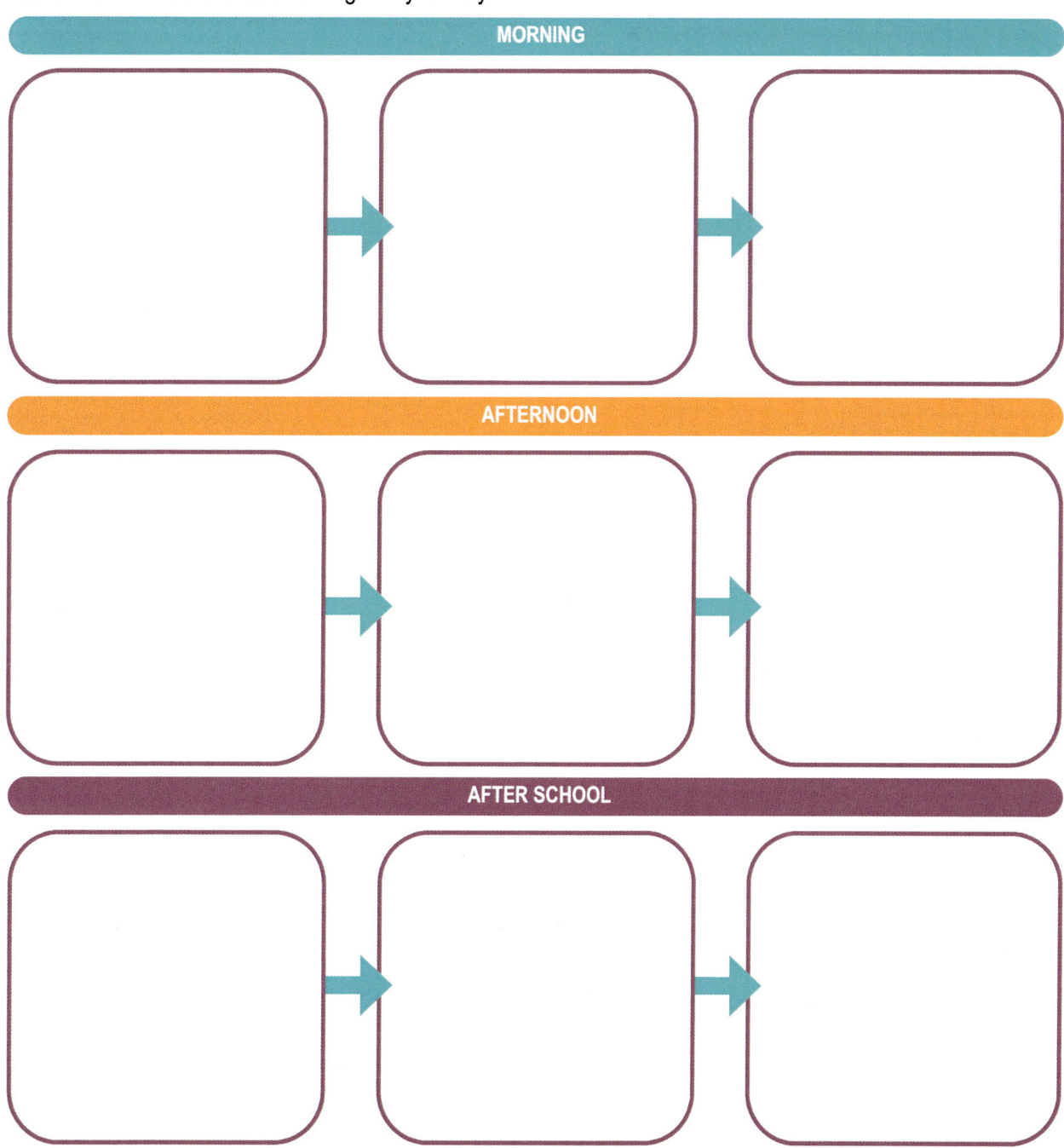

MORNING

AFTERNOON

AFTER SCHOOL

Activity 9

OBJECTIVE

To understand that students with autism have a hard time recognizing personal space.

INSIGHTS

Understanding and respecting personal space helps students to engage more successfully in everyday interactions.

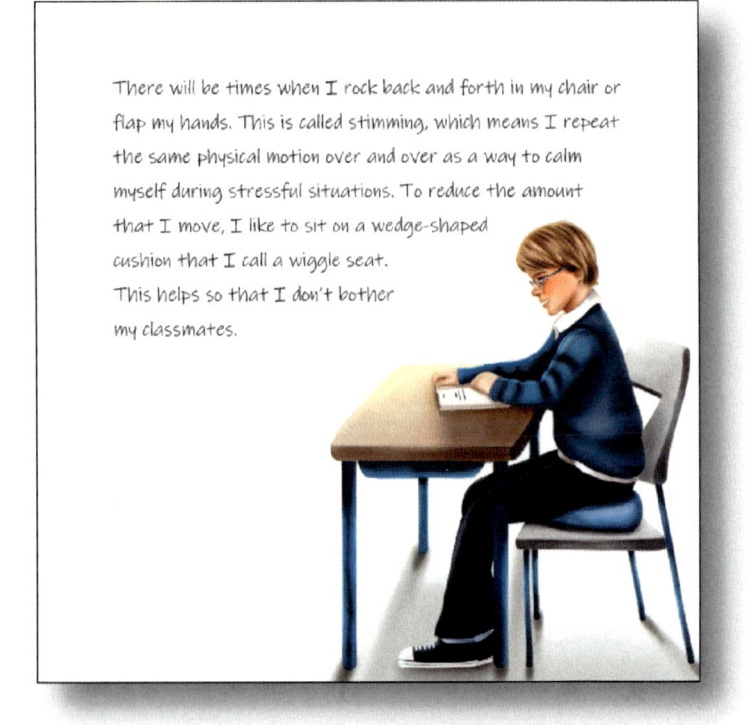

> There will be times when I rock back and forth in my chair or flap my hands. This is called stimming, which means I repeat the same physical motion over and over as a way to calm myself during stressful situations. To reduce the amount that I move, I like to sit on a wedge-shaped cushion that I call a wiggle seat. This helps so that I don't bother my classmates.

EMPATHY PROMPTS

Do you understand what personal space means?

What do you say when you feel like someone is not respecting your space?

How do you respect other people's personal space?

Why do we need our personal space?

POST-ACTIVITY DISCUSSION

Students need to recognize what their personal space is in different situations and how to advocate for themselves if someone intrudes on their space. Depending on the situation, students may need to:

- Back up
- Walk away
- Ask the person to back up or stop touching
- Ask an adult for help

Personal Space

Personal space is the amount of space a person needs to have between themselves and someone else in order to feel comfortable. Cut and paste the choices below in the "good" or "poor" choice columns.

Good Personal Space	Poor Personal Space

- asking before giving a hug
- telling someone they are too close
- grabbing
- walking around people
- touching others in class
- keeping hands to self in line
- climbing on people
- putting your nose on people

Activity 10

OBJECTIVE

To accept that each student learns differently.

INSIGHTS

Understanding that different types of learning styles can impact the way the classroom is set up.

Visual learners learn best when information is presented to them through pictures, graphs or text.

Physical learners learn by "doing".

Auditory learners learn best when information is presented to them orally.

Reading/Writing learners prefer to learn through the written word.

EMPATHY PROMPTS

What kind of learner are you?

Does your teacher know how you learn best?

Is it difficult when the teacher presents information in a format that is not your learning style?

Most days I am called out of the classroom by other teachers and you might wonder why. Sometimes I am practicing reading and other times I am doing writing exercises. I am still learning, just in a different way. It helps me a lot if you let me know what we are working on when I get back!

POST-ACTIVITY DISCUSSION

A classroom should be a place where every student knows they belong and matter. By understanding the different ways in which they learn, students gain a deeper level of understanding and empathy.

Different Ways of Learning

Fill out this chart to understand what type of learner you are. You may have strengths in several areas.

	Always	Sometimes	Never
VISUAL			
I enjoy art and drawing	☐	☐	☐
I learns through images	☐	☐	☐
I am good at making graphs and doing puzzles	☐	☐	☐
PHYSICAL			
I walk around while reviewing information	☐	☐	☐
I like to show rather than tell	☐	☐	☐
I do well with strategy games, computers, and experiments	☐	☐	☐
AUDITORY			
I have excellent memory for names, dates, and trivia	☐	☐	☐
I record lectures to listen to later	☐	☐	☐
I make up songs to memorize something	☐	☐	☐
READING/WRITING			
I read printed information out loud to myself	☐	☐	☐
I look up words I don't know in the dictionary	☐	☐	☐
I take a lot of notes	☐	☐	☐

Made in the USA
Columbia, SC
10 September 2021